Ascension and Return

Ascension and Return

Poetry of a Village Daoist

RENE J. NAVARRO

www.TambuliMedia.com
Spring House, PA USA

First printed on September 20, 2020 by Tambuli Media

ISBN: 978-1-943155-34-7
Library of Congress Control Number: 2020943140

Cover photo ©2020 Laura Billingham Photography
Calligraphy by 陳洪邦 Chan Hung Bond
Designed by Summer Bonne

Tambuli Media
1121 N. Bethlehem Pike #60-179
Spring House, PA 19446

www.TambuliMedia.com

Dedication

For grandfather, Paulino Navarro, Ingkong Poli, raconteur and farmer and artisan, the greatest influence in my early life. Ingkong Poli told me stories of powerful beings, warriors, monsters, fairies, from legends and corridos. It was in this idyllic world that I was first exposed to nature, storytelling, native herbs, craftsmanship, martial arts, poetry, and the mystical.

Praise

"The author's words lift off the page, taking the reader to places you have never been, and some that you have."

—*William Craft, B.S., M.Ed.*

"A full and unique life of study and travel is revealed in this collection from an observant and insightful author. A compelling and enjoyable read..."

—*Dianne Craft, B.A., M.A.T*

"Rene's poetry expresses the inner journey of a mystic in a way that allows the reader to peer into that which is usually hidden. It shows that poetry is an alchemy of words, and alchemy is the poetry of the soul, and both paths are expressed by the words Rene puts to paper. When I read these poems, I am called back to the inner journey that is so easy to forget in modern life, but so essential for all of us."

—*Dr. Henry McCann, DAOM, LAc*

"Rene Navarro is a friend, a teacher, a healer, a seeker on the path, and an adventurer ceaselessly in search of the truth of human potential. His poetry embodies those aspects of his personality and life and carries the reader along on this search for truth and beauty. Take the journey with him."

—*Mike Arsenault, Licensed Acupuncturist*

"I have had the good fortune of working with Rene for 15 years and enjoying his friendship for 25. The amazing breadth of his knowledge of the martial and healing arts is matched by his generosity in sharing it. Through the years his poetry has also been an inspiration. The first works I encountered were from the chapbook "At Dufu's Cottage." What I love most about his writing is the ease of flow of thought, image and feeling."

—*Karen Marie Borla, L.Ac., M.Ac., Dipl. O.M.*

Foreword by Dr. Mark Wiley

The Daoist philosopher Laozi wrote, "*A journey of a thousand miles begins with a single step.*" But when the journey is of a lifetime and extends the world over, an uncountable number of single steps must be taken. The life of Rene Navarro is an example of a lifetime of journeys, travels, training, developing, and learning new skills. It is a lifetime of dedication to self-development and growth in every way.

Rene and I met in letters and telephone around 1992, I think. It seems before this we had heard of one another, or at least I had been familiar with him, as we shared so many of the same friends in the Philippines and USA who were, like us, devoted to the martial arts and healing traditions. My kung-fu master, the late Sifu Alex Co, published a book by the late Edgar Sulite titled, *The Masters of Arnis*, in which Rene was featured. Another mutual friend and Rene's arnis teacher, Amante Marinas, had written about Rene in a magazine which I had read. In 1994, Rene was one of the only people to send in a paid subscription to my short-lived newsletter, *Tambuli*. I was honored, and grateful. Another mutual friend, Halford Jones had mentioned him to me often, so in 1996 when I relocated from Tokyo to Boston while working as Editor for the Charles E. Tuttle Publishing Co., Rene and I were able to finally meet in person. We became instant friends. We shared so many interests and friends. He treated my migraines with acupuncture, we ate well, he became a mentor to me.

After some time, I relocated to Towson, MD and Rene came to visit. By this time, I had a son, Alex, for whom Rene became one of his ninongs (godfathers). I remember Rene playing with him, and cooking for my family and playing some arnis in the living room. He also performed abdominal massage on me and taught me the rudiments of the Six Healing Sounds qigong (*liu zi jue*). Rene is a disciple of Master Mantak Chia and had written several chapters for some of his books. He also helped Vincent Chu edit his Tai Ji book and present it to me to publish, which I did.

Mark Wiley and Rene Navarro in the author's home, standing alongside the Fasting Buddha.

A series of travels and time separated Rene and I for several years, maybe more than a decade. I was back in my hometown of suburban Philadelphia, and I heard that Rene was living north of me in Easton, PA. Again, we connected and caught each other up on our journeys and studies. What a journey Rene had been on from Egypt to Bali to Thailand to Hong Kong and so many more places, visiting masters of martial arts, energy work, and poetry. We have met up several times in the past years for lunch at Daddy's Place in Easton, I inducted him in the Society of Black Belts of America, where he taught a workshop session, and he introduced me to the Traditional Yang Tai Ji and broadsword forms (which I have yet to develop), and has generously shared his qigong skills performing healings on me and my wife, Kellie.

Sitting in Rene's lair, his private space in his home, is a real treat. It is filled with relics and artifacts of his life, his travels, his studies, his family and masters and Gods of many nations. As I sat with him drinking lotus leaf tea one time, I recalled in the 90s that had given me a copy of his self-published poetry book, and later shared a poem of his that was published in the anthology, *Flippin – Filipinos on America*. I then invited Rene to gather his favorite poems and essays into a book for Tambuli Media. He did just that, and here we are, on the approach of Rene's 80th birthday, proud to present to the reader, *Ascension and Return: Poetry of a Village Daoist*. It is the first of several books Tambuli will publish with Rene. From the first entry the reader will fall in love with the author, his work, his insights, his skill, his heart.

Foreword by David Verdesi

Rene has been a teacher and a father figure in my life since we met in 1992. That was 28 years ago! I was barely 16 years old then.

I recall it was just Rene and me in the field in the morning just before dawn, each absorbed in our practice routine. I had been training seriously with several accomplished teachers for several years by this time, and thanks to that experience, I saw immediately that Rene was well above the norm; his skill was of another caliber all together. His demeanor, power, countenance, and elegance attracted me as I waited patiently for him to pause between his training sets.

I approached Rene and saluting in the traditional way with folded hands I asked him if he would be my teacher. He looked at me quietly for a while then he nodded saying, "I don't accept private students lightly, but I've been watching you training. Your basics are quite good, you were lucky to have good teachers. We need to work on foundations and stances more if you want to move your practice to the next level. It is going to be hard and quite repetitive and boring, but if you are ready meet me tonight after dinner..." Well, I was there after dinner and the rest is history.

Countless hours were spent training in stances and moving in drills, routines, and practicing qigong before dawn and again at night. The satisfaction of his nod of approval are precious memories which mingle with the joy of sharing hearty meals together after training.

Nowadays, in the West at least, it is hardly possible to meet a man and a teacher such as Rene Navarro. Such mastery, resilience, dedication, passion, and persistence are the stuff of legend.

The author (left) and David Verdesi right) with Sifu Wang Tin Jun, master of Xing Shen Zhuang and Wu Style Tai Ji Quan, in Chiang Mai, Thailand in 2002.

Less talking, more doing. Goals may change as time ripens us to perfection, but perfect practice is always needed. Not fancy theories just practice every day, two-to-three times a day over a lifetime — not 1 year, not 5 years, not 10 years. A lifetime.

That is who Rene is for me: an example of a lifetime of dedication to the arts he chose to master. Someone who always walked his path with clarity, dignity, courage, and uncompromising passion. I remember him telling me what I now tell my students: "Instead of learning 1,000 new forms and routines practice one to perfection." That is gongfu, that is qigong, that is the essence of the Dao and the De and it is how the De grows within.

Thank you, Rene, my old teacher and friend, through you a young boy glimpsed into a past that is no more and was shaped by you in many ways into the man I am today. Your legacy lives on as I pass the essence of your example to the new generations that will follow. I am forever grateful.

Table of Contents

Tai Ji Quan

do not speak the words
for the gesture
you have to learn
the movement

repeat it
maybe a thousand
times probably more
in silence

the eyes follow
the entry of the hands
into the space

wheeling around
your center

the heart keeps
a slow count
for you
as you breathe
through the pores
of your
skin

the feet reach down
into the earth
and the crown opens

up to the sky
as your mind empties
itself to receive
a benediction
from the stars

and one day it may happen

a rainbow shimmers
just somewhere
between the muscles
the marrow and the blood
deep currents
shooting
down your legs
and arms

there is a
radiance
in your eyes when you feel
for the first time
the pull of earth and sky

and you are in the middle
of this
congruence as you draw
the circles
around you
with your hands

your body listens
becomes
sound and color
and pulsing

and you taste
the beginning
where we came from
and where we shall
all
return

– after reading Luis Cabalquinto's poem, "Alignment"

2

Longhushan Idyll

Doing Ancestor Lu Dongbin's Tai Ji Quan
Sword Dance outside
in mid-Autumn: a deer is watching me
from the edge of the woods
as it sniffs the wind
descending from the west.
A full moon above the pines
but it is playing hide
and seek behind the clouds
and trees. In the valley,
smoke is rising from a thatched hut.
I have been following my routine
of daily meditation since 11 last night,
the first watch
in the Hour of Tzu.
It is just 3 in the morning now
and there is no sound
of human presence here
on Dragon Ridge. The Breatharian
Hermit Xuan Kong
in the Immortal's Cave
on the Eastern slope
has not shown up for days.
I listen for his footfalls but
there is only the rustling
of the wind in the pine trees
and bamboo leaves swirling around me.
A jug of hot black tea is waiting

on a rock. Jiang shifu told me
to sit and meditate and go
into the void. No, shifu, now is not
the time to block everything
from my eyes and ears
and float
in emptiness.
There is so much to feast on
with the senses. Why
go inward now when the earth
is so rich with its colors,
scents, tastes and sounds?
Li Bai, Su Dong Po, Tao Qian,
Du Fu, my mentors and brothers,
let us get together again.
Send for the best turtle soup,
deer tendon casserole,
West Lake carp, Shanghai
crab and chrysanthemum
flowers.
Let us get drunk
on the best Lanling wine
and ride the dragon chariot
on the Milky Way.

3

In West Lake, after Bai Juyi

I look at my image in the water
at Xihu: in the mirror of the lake
I see an old man, bearded, hair
thinning and grey, face marked
with deep worry lines on the forehead,
beside the eyes, along the cheeks.
70 years. How much longer
will I be here on this earth?
I walk up Baopu Temple and halfway
I stop to rest. I listen to my breath
and my heart, wipe the sweat
on my brows with my palm.

I too have lost my youth, my friend,
And I shall never find it again.*

How did Ge Hong do it?
Ten years ago I jogged up
these steps to the top, without
stopping, bowed to the altar
and looked down
on the red dragon on the roof.
Now, I hear my lungs wheezing,
my knees buckling under my own weight,
my eyesight fading. My friends
are all gone now. I, alone, remain
and I remember the time when
we used to stay up all night, drinking

the cheap wine in Sichuan, and
singing songs of the hills,
nibbling on pig's heart
and chicken feet.

*Bai Juyi's poem

4

Sword Dance in the Moonlight

How did you do it, Li Bai?
Turning your back on the court,
Endlessly wandering
The kingdom, fleeing to those
Crags of mountains inhabited
By deer, scorpions and tigers.
You watch the full moon
In an empty sky, a wine-gourd
Beside you, and write these
Lines you set, like peach blossoms,
On the flowing river. You whip your sword
Flashing with moonlight: I hear
The ping of dragon steel trailing
In the pines. Movements of sword
Dance: Circles of phoenixes flying
In the night, floating gossamer
Scarves of silk. Here, in
Du-Fu's retreat, your laughter
Trembles with the water on the
Pond. I see the shimmer of your
Voice, bouncing from reflecting
Pool to green bamboo leaves,
From wooden bridge to the
Stupa on the hill.

At Baopu Temple, Xihu, Hangzhou

Last year you bowed
under the Tai Ji sign
at the foot of the hill
before we climbed
up to light candles
at the altar
above West Lake.
Now, this early morning
at the Hour of the Tiger
I walk the dirt road
to Baopu Temple and feel
your absence. On a hill nearby
Buddhist monks are chanting
sutras, the reverberations
echoing across the waters
to the pagodas in the distance.
As I pass the rock where we sat,
I catch a glimpse of you
In white doing
the Immortal Sword Dance
in the darkness.
There is a spark of lightning
in the sky and thunder
rolling down West Lake.
I hear the Golden Rooster
crowing among the pines
ready to fly to Heaven.
I light 3 joss sticks for you

as the Daoist priest
rings a gong
at the Dragon Gate.
Where
is Ge Hong,
the alchemist,
can he do his magic
to bring you back
here among the willow
trees?

6

Li Bai in West Mountain

A restless night.
My head still heavy
with wine.
Half-awake,
half-asleep,
I see the battlefield
covered with the dead
and the dying
at the borderlands.
Blood soaks the ground.
Fear stalks
the land
of my ancestors.
My fingertips frozen
as I embrace my sword.
A long wrestling
match with
the ghosts
at midnight.
The wind
is moaning
against the willow trees
in the valley.
The hut is shaking.
The chimes
are trembling
in the dark.

7

Tao Yuan-Ming from his Hermitage

The chrysanthemum blooms
even in autumn. The lotus grows
in the muck. The bamboo bends
when the wind blows. The plum bears
fruit in winter. The orchid thrives
although it hangs on a tree, its roots
altogether detached from the earth.
What do we do to survive?
What is essential, what is enough
to bring us life? The hermit lives
on air and mist and light and wild yam.
How much do we really need in life?
Why do we accumulate all these
possessions, indulge the senses, and lose
our way on the road? We carry
this baggage on our shoulders
and our hands are always full,
a closet bursting at the seams.
I gave up my government job
for a farm and solitude and poetry.
I love the laughter
of children and the sounds
of cattle and birds, and the warmth
of friends around me.
What else is there to seek?

8

Meditation

Seize me and circle:
Phoenix and Dragon together,
Enter into my navel. Enter.

O what Joy stirs
in my loins, deep,
deeper. Into the bones
Hissing: O radium light
Descending. Into the
Soul's meridians
Burning. Diabolus
of Pearl ascending.
It orbits the Heavens
now, bright, brighter.
It floats to Earth again:
Dark and still darker,
Here, there, pulsing.

O Radiance, I'm falling.
Ambushed, helpless, lost
Between ecstasy and dying.

– for Jose Garcia Villa

9

Dragon

Snow is falling in transparent
sheets across the garden
of lilacs into the woods
beyond. The dragon is out
there, his tail whipping
the wind in gusts
along the rhododendron path.
He has been out since
dawn, tasting the melting
snow on his tongue. He hears
the elegant explosion
of a flake vaporizing
in an instant: it recalls
other quiet
revelations
of the quotidian…

…Flute
music rising with the mist above
the darkening canopy
of trees in a deep
valley somewhere in
the Catskills where Rip
Van Winkle slept
for 20 years.

The morning
sun in haze as the rays hit the air
descending on Chengdu from the foothills
of the Himalayas.

The taste of cold
ripe cherimoya: sweet,
sour, bitter
at once, flavors
of a childhood
in a tropical
town north
of Manila.

The moaning
echoes of a frozen Waban
Lake as ice pushed
against ice…

All the seasons
of his lifetimes
he has heard
this earthsong as
of white cranes taking him
to the farthest
star, his senses
waking him
in small
satori to the presence
of God on earth.

10

Ascension

Is it true you drowned
Embracing the moon in the
Lake at Kunming? I believe
You flew to the Western Shore
The moon in one hand
A flask of wine in the other
Trailed by Du Fu who was
Himself drunk: Two white
Cranes, Li Bai, you and Du Fu
Rising from the still water,
Flapping your wings in silence,
Twin lights ascending
To the North Star,
Gateway to Heaven.

Return

"Reversal is the way of the Dao." — Laozi, *Dao De Jing*

We gaze in stillness at the dark
blue night in Chongqing and trace
the fading footsteps that we have taken
in this life, and the many lifetimes
on this planet. In the geography
of ancient towns and cities, we look
for the streams back to our birth,
each day like a wave on the Huangzi
as it ebbs into the sea,
its inhabitants of newborn eels
coming up for air, cormorants deep
in the water, blue herons standing
like statues on the shore, a rare
green parrot lost from an aviary
downstream, and we step on the map
of memory into time, beyond the slow corruption
of our bodies, our minds, our souls
to our infancy, and further back,
past the fusion of cells, bones and flesh,
past this earth and other stars,
into oblivion and further back,
past Atlantis and the lost continents,
past the invention of boundaries, and weapons,
and the human devices
of wealth, and fame, and status
and distinctions, that have split us

from within and from each other, past the poisons
of the millenniums, beyond the Milky Way
to the beginning, inch by inch, drop
by drop, on the eternal river,
where we'll find the source,
the spring, of the self, breath that's pure
genetrix, primal energy, uncorrupted,
fresh, immortal, to that luminous
and peaceful dawn in the landscape
of eternity, back to the umbilicus,
back to the navel
and the very womb of the Dao.
Ziran.

– after reading Mark Frutkin's poem, "Reinventing the World"

12

Cheng Du Dawn

Still awake, bats
Fly over the dark river
And a crescent moon.

They descend toward
The moon again and again
As if to touch it.

Beside the willows
An old woman draws circles
Summoning silence.

Her fingers stroke
Lute strings and peacock tails
In the damp warm air.

The woman listens
To the beginnings of light
In her flesh and bones.

Come, watch the ritual:
She unreels the Dao in silk
From cocoons of mist.

Deep in her navel
A votive candle flickers:
A flaming odalisque!

– for Len Roberts

13

Dragon

I rehearse death every chance I get.
Slowly I turn my eyes inward
to summon the dragon from his lair.
I wait for him to move, speaking to him only
with my mind. He has to be stirred gently
for flight every day at midnight when
it is quiet and the skies are clear of aircraft.
This dragon does not breathe fire, he's
too lazy to move from sleep, he has
been coiled for centuries. I bribe him with
a pearl that shines in the dark. I follow
his trajectory in space. He flies
among the leaves of the sycamore in
my backyard, plays with the light of the
moon reflected on the wet grass. Mine
is a young dragon, reincarnated a few times.
He's full of anger yet, unresolved karma
from a previous life. Lustful too for
women's flesh, who knows why.
I make him fly higher and farther
from my house, not too far though since he
is still too weak for distance runs.
Now I pull him back on his leash,
a really tired dragon needing rest.

14

North Star in Doi Saket

The early morning breeze
carries the scent of grass
burning in the fields.
On a hill nearby,
Buddhist priests
are chanting
sutras as I practice
my Tai Ji sword
under the ancient map
of an indigo sky.
I toss a strand of qi
to the North Star.
I toss another one.
I keep tossing
my qi through
the tip of my dragon
sword, like sending
a pigeon with a
message home. Only silence
and the mountains
in the distance.

15

Company

Early morning in Brooklyn:
My children, Al and Norman,
6 and 9, and Lolit, my wife, are still
asleep. I take the elevator
down to the lobby
and go out into the dark,
carrying my rattan
sticks for my martial practice at 5
in the park. Unseasonably warm
in late October. Nobody
around, only a couple
of joggers in the oval.
A mist paints a gray
efflorescence over the handball
and tennis courts where I stand
facing a graffitied wall to do
a thousand strikes of sinawali,
a hundred abecederos with
my right hand, a hundred
with my left, chanting
my Pilipino mantras
"agos," "kumpas" and "indayog
ng katawan," thinking
of the images that these words
evoke— a river flowing,
a syncopated beat,
and a cobra ready
to strike— and I repeat

the routine 2 or 3 times more
in silence before the sun
comes up, until I break
into a sweat, feel
an exquisite
ache shooting
through my arms,
legs and chest, and I come
back from a tropical island,
where I had as my guide
and company
the warrior
Lapu-Lapu, who slew
Ferdinand Magellan, April
1521.

– for Norman F. Navarro, MD

Island Shaman

I lie on my stomach
in the dark and feel
the old man's bony
hands probing
the muscles on my back.

Island shaman, guru,
herbalist, warrior, priest:
He knows,
with his
callused fingers
where the hurt
hides
trapped
between
the folds of flesh,
there where
the shoulder
blades meet, behind
the heart.

He presses
the spine,
chasing the
tangle
of nerves from
the spot. He knows,

he who can see the color
of pain, read
from the texture
of my pulse
what anguish is wrapped
around me like emanations
of heat
from the earth
after
a summer rain.

My eyes closed, I see
layers of anger
over grief over hate
over fear fleeing
from his touch.
I smell his breath
heavy with the odor
of native cigar.

I lose him briefly
and as I awake
I see his
teeth dark
from nicotine
and tar
and the spittle
on the corners
of his mouth.
He is reciting
ancient mantras
of the island. Passing
an amulet

over me,
he mumbles
an exorcism
in the dark.

– for Guiling Tinga

17

At the Nursing Home with Dad

In Memoriam: Ricardo Y. Navarro
January 15, 1916 – December 31, 2001

I was visiting alone. Eighth floor, in his room
overlooking the valley. On the bulletin board
a note: RYN/Speech Therapy. Daddy,

Daddy, I said, you had speech therapy
today, what did you do? They did all
the talking, he stuttered. They did

all the talking, he giggled, and kept mumbling
this line of mantra that seemed to echo
in the distant autumn hills of Rockland

while my mind raced back to my first year
in high school, 13 years old, and even now
I can still taste the slice of raw ginger

he told me to suck on while he and I
are at the grandstand and he is teaching me
public speaking, he is telling me

to raise my voice, but not to shout, to keep it
deep and low, to let it come from the belly,
as I recited a passage from Clarence

Darrow's speech defending a union
leader, my father saying louder,
louder, I can't hear you, I can't hear you

in the half-dark from 30 feet below.

18

Dream on Wat Phra That Doi Suthep

I'll sound your name on the ancient bells
in the temple of Doi Suthep.
I'll write your name on a gold leaf and press it
on the Buddha's heart as he sits in prayer in the sun.
I'll whisper your name to the petals of the lotus flower
that I'll offer to the altar beside the incense
smoke rising like dragons and phoenixes to the sky.
It is my way of worship: the way I hold your
face now in my hand like a piece of raw wet jade
picked from the river, the way I step
into sacred space with my bare feet, the way
I rest my head on your thighs.

- for G

19

Dream on Huashan

I know I'll never be able
to touch you. I'll never
be able to know how it is
to pass my fingers
over your skin, the fuzz
on your nape and arms.
I'll never be able to press
my tongue over the curve
of your neck down to your
shoulder and the folds
of your armpit. Since you are
vowed to another man,
you won't allow this desire
to touch you. So you sit
and contemplate the throbbing
of your veins, the pulsing
of your heart and the ache
on your temples. I know
I'll have to keep the distance
between us even as we walk
side by side, even as we
move in the same room,
avoiding each other's
eyes. Here, in this temple
in the eastern peak
shrouded with white mist
our breath is frozen.
From across the room

we travel to the Center,
under the great beams,
over the meditation rock,
halfway between the rafters
and the cold stone floor.
You a nun vowed
to a dead man and I,
a priest, following
the Right Hand Path.

– for CW

20

Thinking of Li Bai

In my wanderings, I think
of my mentor and friend Li Bai
every now and then,
wishing I had his company.
But after the armies
of empire
began massing along
the frontiers of a foreign
land, and the loud rhetorics
of battle filled the air,
he went
into seclusion
again. Away he went,
to quiet
his heartmind, write weary
poems
he would drop, like
peach
blossoms, on the flowing
stream. He would watch
the golden phoenixes,
and white cranes
riding the green wind,
listen for the crow
of heaven's rooster,
await the loud peal
of thunder,
mourn

the useless deaths
of young warriors,
lament the horror
and anguish
of war,
I don't know
which it is now.
Is he in Tiantaishan,
among the immortals
toasting the elixir
of life?
He did not say
goodbye, he did not
say goodbye, just
disappeared
from the way
of man.

-for BR

21

Memory

Waking
up in the empty dark-
ness of a bamboo hut
somewhere
in the hills far
from the old home-
town: At three, that's
the first picture
in my memory.
Alone, without
a blanket
on a cold morn-
ing, the sharp
passage of a fighter
plane, and wet
pants.

A month or two
later, perhaps a year,
a vegetable
patch on the side
of a hill and an under-
ground cave dug in the red
earth
for if the shooting
came. There were green
painted rattan
furniture, a sofa and

chairs, I can still see
them. And farther back earlier,
a bamboo and nipa hut on the side
of a mountain and vegetables
growing.
Perhaps it was
later: there was
the burst of light
from a cannon
and the resonant
blast following.
There are no
clear faces, just objects
and places and sounds
and the long
walk barefoot on a rough,
hot road
with my older cousins
Dan and Letty
to the camp
where a Japanese
sergeant always fed
us a bowl of rice
soup.

Still later, towards
the end of the war,
my mother calling

my brothers and me
across the field
to eat the yams

she cooked
with a thick coat-
ing of melted brown
sugar.

In this landscape
I did not
know who
was fighting, why

the bombardment and the
dogfights in the sky.

I couldn't read
the signs
saying Japan or America,
which cannon or plane
belonged
to which side.
But the fear
I knew.

The fear remains
50 years later.

The Old Calligrapher

His pink kimono split the sun
Into a thousand rays: white cranes
Homing to his onyx eyes. He sat
In a full lotus on the meditation
Pillow, smiling, pale lips
Pressed to hide the smile, and
Remembering the girl in spring
Long ago in this stone garden.
He had given her a scroll of rice
Paper with a pictograph
Of the sun rising and a sketch of
Cherry blossoms gently
Falling. As she bowed, she slipped a
Phoenix-and-dragon
Ring into his priestly robe and
Left him to the Sunday crowd
That gathered to watch his work.
He glanced at the island
Mountains: five sacred peaks
In a sea of raked
Sand. He breathed deeply,
Drawing the landscape
In his mind. In a
Flash his eyes turned to
Gold, the islands and the sea
Eddied and glowed. And he was
Gone. Like washed ink,
His shadow in meditation remained

Etched on the bleached rock:
The first calligraphy of his
Death.

23

Bilocation

I am touring the White House
and I see the US soldiers
marching
home leaving a country
of dead bodies
men, women, children
over ten. The bamboo flutes
and kulintang broken
by the wayside,
the krises and kampilans
taken for memorabilias
and museums. And I am there
a young survivor hiding
in the forest. Nothing
to play with, nobody
to tell me the stories
of the ancestors, nothing
left except the bibles,
cans of spam and the
comic books of the
conqueror.

24

Sulu

Child, you are pushing with your frail arms
A cart in the ruins of your hometown
Bombed by your own countrymen.

Child, you snatched a world out of the flames:
A rusty nail, a pot or a can:
In the wreckage of the present
Or the past, or the future, which?

I can't see your eyes in the eerie smoke
But I know they burn with fear and anger
Since that night the mercenaries of the fascist
Regime swept down from the skies
Flying death-machines marked U.S. on their wings.

Now every day you watch and run
When the dark cross-shadow of a plane passes by.
You listen to the rumors of flight, the distant formations
Above the dark clouds of your isles.

You wonder, as you pick this hammer, that screw,
At the hellfire far away belched by napalm bombs
That rained beauty and death on your land.

25

A Boat on the Nile

The patient, a dark woman
whose looks do not tell her age
or history, lies on her belly
crying on the makeshift
treatment table. The acupuncture
needles vibrate on her back,
along the outer meridians
that reveal the secret
wounds she suffered
in life, and suppressed.
Outside the window
her husband is hovering back and forth,
in an eternal ritual of the patriarchy, making
his presence felt, mad that he was asked
to leave. For an hour,
she does not stop
crying. She clutches
the black shawl, dark
as her grief.
She does not say
a word. How can one have all
that grief in the world? Pain
that speaks in the hieroglyphs
of tears. Pain
from years enduring
the beatings and his
alcoholism, the abuse
written on her bones

as ancient as the pyramids,
the tears flowing, quiet
and deep
as the waters
of the Nile,
its waves
rocking us
below
just now.

Chichen Itza, Mexico

The earth's deep pool
Receives the sacrifice:

Water bursts, bubbles,
Explodes in a scream:

Gold and flesh
Sink to the depths
Together.

The Serpent God descends
The stairs of the Pyramid.

27

At Marble Collegiate Church with Marla and Donald

I was listening
to the Very Reverend
Norman Vincent Peale
as he spoke
about the power
of faith as small
as a mustard
seed, but I couldn't sit
still, I kept
sneaking a look
at Marla,
itching to
play with her,
touch the tips
of her fingers,
see her navel
under that silk,
but Donald
was watching
by her side,
a sharp-eyed
dog guarding
his trophy,
as we sat
in a balcony
pew along
with others,

and so my restless Daoist
spirit
fled to the rafters
and the stained glass
windows while
my meridians
and vortices
were flashing
lights and colors,
eddies and trajectories
of energy
in the dark, oozing
like the aurora
borealis, and
the preaching voice
was gone.
I was on my own,
my shell of a body
was left
on the seat
clutching
a purple hymnal,
while I flew
off into space
with the
8 Immortals.

28

Mattapoisett Neck Beach Spring Equinox Morning

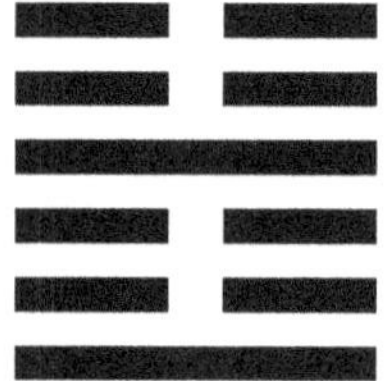

Hexagram 51
Zhen
Taking Action
Thunder above
Thunder below

we walked to the end
of the beach
by this inland sea
with the wind
blowing hard
on our backs
we made
our way
beside the wet
seaweeds
to taste this spring
equinox morning
after a night
of thunder
and rain

you tightened
the drawstring
on my hood

to keep the chill
off my ears your hands
were so small

it is still
winter I said
and gave
you my pair
of black
mittens to wear
over your unmatched
gloves

boot prints marked
the path ahead on the
edge of the salt
marsh

the sea was coming
in with the cold breeze in gusts
across the breakers
a silent seagull
surveyed the cove from above
gray profile on gray

the dark cormorants
were not at their island rock
waiting not this time

there was no bell ringing no
fisherman's dinghy bobbing
beside the buoy

the sand bar where
we were nearly trapped
by the rising tide
last autumn
was just a
silhouette beneath
the waves and
the random rocks
we stepped on to get
to it were hardly jutting
above the water

this wasn't what
we wanted but we
braved the winter
weather to reach
the far end

as we did
many times
before

near the end
of the beach the sand
had been washed
away leaving
a bed
of sharp rocks
on the high watermark

a stream was flowing now
where a dry bed was
stained dark green and black
at its source were
stumps of trees in the distance

we couldn't sit
on the last
outcropping where
we used to soak
up the summer sun
we were freezing
from the wind
stirring farther
somewhere
in the mainland

walking back I noticed
how far
we had gone

with the wind
on our faces
the distance
seemed
greater
this time

- for MS

29

A Clearing in the Sky

Although the sky
is still dark and the May
clouds threaten another
downpour, the rain
has briefly stopped
for the outdoor
wedding
to begin, and I watch
my son Albert
in his transparent
pina barong Pilipino
waiting by the altar of fresh cut
branches and dogwood trees
while his Laura all radiance
and hope marches on her father's
arm down the aisle of grass
to the music
of the brass band and the cackling
of the peacocks and guinea hens
in the barn,
and I see him,
6 years, in Prospect Park
running and turning
back and laughing,
black hair flying,
bright eyes
blazing with the morning
as he pulls the string

of the red kite, its long white
tail trailing, as it ascended
like a Zhu Bei Hong horse,
trembling against the wind,
the greening
trees and meadows
spinning
around him, the tenements
and the city
traffic dissolving
in the Spring sun,
as his stallion cantered, sniffed
the grass and air,
floated and glowed
in the Stillness,
a tracery
of Light,
eternal, pulsing
in the clear blue
space
that opens
between
earth
and sky.

– for Al and Laura

30

Clearing the Life

December 3, 1993, 5 am:
at the end
of the year
I try to get
my bedroom
in order. With each
day, it seems to get
smaller. It's too
crowded now, there
is too little space
to move, I have
to tiptoe around odds
and ends stacked
randomly everywhere. I am
clearing junk mail, scraps,
old newspaper
clippings, notes and
reminders posted
on a Styrofoam board. On my desk
are all sorts of things: along
with my dragon chop from
Sichuan, a glue stick,
slide viewer, cups, pens
that have dried, vitamins I don't
even take. What is
junk, what is not?
Why do we keep some
things at all?

I've been looking
at each item piled
inside boxes and stuff
comes out and feels
heavy on my back as I
swim through
the day. Here are notes
from a previous
life. There is a journal
from 1970 with
aphorisms, quotes
from books I read, thoughts
on exile and my first
autumn in the US.
I know I don't need
them, but I couldn't
let them go like the first
draft of letters on my computer.

I can't even remember why
they are here
buried under other things in no
particular sequence, each
like a claim on my time.
I hold this rock with veins
of crystal and I can't remember
when I picked it up from
what beach: it must
have been beautiful
on the surf shiny and wet;
now, it feels warm in my hands
but yields no more memories than
much of what gathers dust on the
windowsill. I know as I get older

I need these things even less.
Many that I enjoyed before
are now dead weights. These things
have piled up in baskets
and drawers and chairs
like the petty worries
that distracted me
as I walked in the meadow
for fresh air.

How much do I really need
to bring with me when
my lease is up
and I move away
from here?

I wonder what
Sakyamuni Buddha
thinks from his perch
atop my corner
bureau where
he quietly observes
my comings and goings
in this piece of crowded
earth.

Quite a few of these
have given me
pleasure, times
when I seemed
to descend through
the dark and found a
place to rest instead. A few
tell of times with friends

who made the journey easier, some
are maps of places
I have been to and places
I like to be. But what do I keep
a map of Paris for
or Brooklyn, places
I may not see
again? Some of these things
I will give away to people
who I hope will embrace
them as I have like
Ursa Major and Ursa Minor,
teddy bears above
my bed. Many of them
I will have to throw
away: rough copies of
printouts, those old Times
on the rack...

Make space
for my life.

12/7/93, Weston, MA, 4:45 AM

31

Watching the Incense Burn: Instructions for a Devotional

Today, it is two joss sticks for us.
Yesterday it was one: for the Wu-Ji,
the One, where everything is birthed, even
Time and Space
and Eternity. Tomorrow,
it will be three, for the Trinity
of Heaven, Earth and Humanity
and the Three Treasures of the body.
In the dark, the two sandalwood incense
are like a pair
of eyes glowing, hardly giving
out any light as I am seated
in a half-lotus right
in front of Guanyin's altar.
The two flicker as the ash
falls inside the brass dragon urn.
Smoke coils up from each stick,
souls liberated from matter,
Yin and Yang reaching out
to each other, embracing
as they rise, white plumes touching
the Goddess of Mercy. After the three,
there are the 10,000 Things,
the Myriad Objects in the world.
No incense here: it is the prayers
you offer, the life you live,
your destiny in the present

incarnation. You are
the incense
burning,
the return
back
to the
One.

32

Treating Father with Acupuncture

Lying in bed at the shelter, during
the first of his three strokes, Father looks
at me puzzled, and opens his mouth
to speak but no words come out
and he shakes his head in anger
and defeat. I tell him I'm going
to give him a treatment and show him
the needles in my bag. He smiles
as I press a point on his head
and winces as I insert one needle
on his crown, another on his forehead
between his brows,
two on the webbing of his thumbs
and big toes. He keeps quiet
as I finish that stage of the treatment
and he leans back, sinks his head
on the pillow and naps.
I hear his labored breathing, the cobwebs
heavy on his lungs, and feel the cold
sweat of the loose skin on his face. I palpate
around the misshapen navel and sense
the emptiness there as if a void
had opened in the earth. I rub his feet
with ginseng oil and notice the ingrown
nails and thick calluses on his toes. He knows
I'm here to make him well, but doesn't
understand why I'm needling certain points.
He doesn't realize I'm trying

to retrieve his speech, nourish his pulse
and activate his brain, make
his left arm move, restore his balance,
and when I pull on the fine,
thin needle like a golden thread,
I am hoping, praying,
to call him back
from the labyrinth
where spirits inhabit
the world.

33

The Red Clock

The spring morning bursts
through a prism of pa-kua
crystal.
Here in my mountain retreat,
I hear the wind
and the chimes.

But it is your long golden
hair I am thinking about
draped
carelessly over
my chest. Outside
our tiny room, the traffic
of footsteps
and voices sounded
too loud in the tiny garden
in Doi Saket
that summer.
There was no music
then, no Il Canto di Lama

or Tibetan Singing bowls,
that was later, only
our breathing
in the warm afternoon,
our bodies
getting used to each other,
astonished

at the discovery of close-
ness, our own inner alchemy
of silence. That's what
I remember,

and the red
clock ticking
on my desk.

-for G

34

Drawing the Characters: Ars Poetica

2 am and I am writing more characters
in my notebook with a pentel pen.
There are verticals and horizontals
and diagonals … and drops and slides
and strokes I do not know the Chinese names
for. I study the length of this line, it's longer
than the one above it. This line starts
hanging from a vertical, that one ends
where one line begins. Another
begins at the eaves of a roof. I start over
again and feel the pressure
on the pen and how it varies the shade
of the ink, a little darker here, little lighter
there, thicker here, thinner there.
The proportion strikes me for the first
time, and balance, nothing weighted
down, nothing leaning this way
or that … I know I do not see
the perspective of the whole
character yet, not even each
drop. I notice that I have to learn
what it means to be light, to spread
the ink evenly like they show
in the manual I am following.
Repetitions, repetitions, as my teachers
used to tell me when I was training
in Shaolin and Tai Ji Quan: imitate and
follow, repeat the way master did

the movement and I did each
a hundred times, two hundred,
until my sweat dripped to the floor
of the old Buddhist Temple in Binondo.
Now each page of my sketchbook is covered
with squiggles. There are no erasures,
no corrections. I can only start all
over again. I know a lot
more now. But I do not even have
an idea what ground I have yet to cover.
How about the Qi that each line
should manifest? How about the Shen?
How about the Life
that breathes through each stroke?
How did the ancients
write with brush and ink?

– Hangzhou, China 2004

35

Renga of Rene and Nadine

(1)
The black bear has upset the garbage bin again:
like a thief it came, like a ghost it went.

(2)
Wooden clapper, metal tubes: still and silent
Until the wind blows nightsong through.

(3)
With the winter wind blowing, the pipes shake like bones
in the dark, as I listen to the footfalls of an invisible beast.

(4)
Damp earth soaks up his hot retreat.
All is whispered, but this memory of sound.

(5)
Memory is all we keep — of fear and love and pain.
The keepsake echoes earth, lake and woods retain.

(6)
By the edge of the water, a yellow bird, black beaked
Perches, waiting, head tilted at the dawn breaking overhead.

(7)
Yellow, golden bird: bright harbinger of light.
Your song brings the sun out of the clouds.

(8)
The sky seems to ripple in the morning wind
Mirroring the movement on the water of fish below.

(9)
It is an ancient trout: yellow, green, red, and blue.
Its sinuous body rainbowing colors in the dawn sun.

(10)
He darts beneath a lotus leaf and nibbles on the stem.
Light, dark, light, pass his calm unblinking eyes.

(11)
Above the waters of the bluegreen mountain lake a blue heron
rising: its flight hardly rippling the surface dappled with light.

(12)
Into the thin air, he, swift and soundless, bears a message
To the emperor of the high wind: green growing blue sky.

(13)
His wings lift him above the pines and the oaks and maples
In magical ascension: his body dissolving in the autumn sun.

(14)
At a certain height, a heron can forget he is bird apart.
He stretches his stick legs back and believes he is running.

(15)
A most difficult thing but God does that, too, sometimes:
run instead of fly just to feel how it is to be a mere human.

(16)
God, heron, lake fish, unseen beast, black bear in the bin, merging.
I remember this wholepiece solitude when all beings come together.

(17)
Last night, in the halo of headlights, two deer nibbling the grass.
Today, hunters wearing camouflage are sneaking into the woods.

(18)
They smell of metal and fire, woolen caps covering their heads.
Orange feelings leak from their eyes and they laugh at themselves.

(19)
I wondered what happened to the deer who nibbles at the grass.
Or to the mythic bear who kept upending the garbage bin for food

(20)
What do they make of us, two-legged creatures who smell of fear?
The deer now hanging over a mantle, and the bear, a rug on the floor?

(21)
I see Isabel walking on the shore of the misted lake, all 28 pounds of her,
Hands clasped behind her, eyes staring at birds shrieking in the distance.

(22)
When we see what exists, and we verify with our senses what is
Sometimes our minds slip back and look for what was, what has been lost.

(23)
It is a human trait, this journey back and forth, from the future to the past,
from the past to the future and the elusive present: what's there to salvage?

(24)
The matter of proportion and the issue of timing, these weigh most in action and inaction. When to move and how far?

(25)
I look up and there's a crescent moon in the sky,
I look within and the same moon shines in the dark.

(26)
The white of that moon against the darkness within
Presses away my hungers and cools my blood.

(27)
A woman who, in silence, quenches the thirst of the heart,
And soothes the anguish of the lonely search for the deep life.

(27a)
Beneath the darkness a quiet river flows
spinning into the navel of the granite rock.

(28)
Eyesight failing, so turn within where the view is a partial mirror
Of the path before you, a squirrel, nervous, and the green green iguana.

(29)
Close to the heart of stillness where the senses cannot go,
the pathways disappear and a whole universe pulses with life.

(30)
From the smallest and emptiest room of thought can burst
Open strength and courage to last a lifetime of struggle.

(31)
Strength and courage, as small as the mustard seed of faith,
that spark fire as they encounter life's dark granite rock.

(32)
A pile of dried leaves stirs in the breath of wind, changes shape
When each leaf settles again, it has lost its beginning place.

(33)
What was the face we had in the beginning, before there was an I,
What was the shape of the leaf before it drifted in the autumn wind?

(34)
Pin a moment down, wrestle from it its truth and watch,
As you catch your breath, the shape of fact shifts and changes.

(35)
The chimes are quiet at dusk, the breeze is still like the woods.
It's the silence of flux, the moment before anything stirs on earth.

(36)
Time, not a circle, but a spiral, moving up and around an axis
So that tomorrow, we will meet again.

36

Meditating on Ganesha

A statue of Ganesha (also known as Ganapatei among His 108 names) stands at the temple entrance, a gate that seems to have been riven down the middle leaving 2 identical but opposite pieces like yin and yang. A checkered cloth of black and white patterns is wrapped around statues and trees to embody the concept of good and evil, that one should be aware of its existence and must take care. The people are aware that spirits, good and bad, inhabit the world so miniature baskets called canang sari are offered to the land, the rivers, the trees (especially the giant banyan of Buddha fame), the mountains. The volcanoes too are propitiated, their spirits becalmed, so that there won't be any angry destructive explosions. Trees, depicted with the roots above and the branches below in paintings, are the earth's bridge to heaven, our connection to the divine, the older and higher, the better. Twice or thrice every single day, the people would carry these baskets, some as small as your palm, or even smaller, filled with flowers, rice, art works of coconut leaves, and offer them at an altar or the base of a wall, a granite rock, the edge of a statue. Watch out: you might be stepping on a miniature palm weaving on the ground.

We are alone here. Perhaps the rains in January have kept the tourists away from this open-air temple. It is empty of human presence except for me, my friend Marina,* and a young barefoot girl who is being trained to introduce the landmarks and tell their history. Our guide is wearing a handmade sarong of batik cloth with its swirling colors of the land and the other world, a translucent blouse of coconut fibers, yellow gold sash around her waist and a white frangipani blossom on her ear. A priestess leading a tour of her domain.

As the breeze whips the mist across the landscape, we stand in front of the dark granite Ganesha, the elephant God with a broken tusk, seated in a half-lotus on a block of stone. I wonder about Him, this strange deity who is half-animal, half-human, wielding an axe. Marina inquires about the rat, Ganesha's equally storied and symbolic mount. The girl says it is somewhere. She bows in worship, palms together in ritual reverence, steps forward and lifts the corner of the checkered cloth wrapped around the waist of Ganesha: there is the tiny rat hiding at the base of the statue. In the rain and the cold, it is the best place to be.

We walk through puddles in the compound as the rain gets heavier. We retreat to a hut overlooking the deep valley and a distant active volcano spewing steam from its caldera. Another mystical symbol, like Sun and Moon, among many: water in a cauldron of fire, the image of ancient alchemy. I hear the Balinese girl talking about the Ring of Fire, volcano after volcano across the 14,000 islands, as we shiver under the roof of palm leaves.

I, a Filipino, am hearing for the first time stories about Ganesha and His long list of attributes. He could be found at the gate of the 5000 temples that you'll see everywhere in this small tropical island. A mysterious mythology I am not used to: a zoomorphic representation of godhood and beginnings and entrances, He removes obstacles to new enterprises. At the same time, He plants challenges along the way to test us and make us strong. He insures safe passage. Whatever it is we do, we always begin. All these thoughts were streaming as we sheltered from the rain in a corner of the temple.

On the ceiling of the Sistine Chapel in the Vatican, God the Father is represented as muscular beefed-up Hercules, looking like an Italian superhero, index finger animating an equally muscular Adam. In other old cultures, the divine is incarnated as a crocodile or a dragon, or thunder and lightning. The Almighty has to assume an earthly face, not some abstract being, something familiar to us so that we could understand it better. In Bali, there is one God but with different manifestations and each one has a recognizable form. The earth itself, and everything in it, is sanctified! As I contemplate this thought I hear the Balinese girl's voice through the mist. I have to interpret her words to explain the paradoxes and profusion of images of an ancient religion. I am adopting a new (for me) hermeneutics: Ganesha's animal features like His large head, big belly, long trunk, big ears and others represent wisdom, the divine and the earth, the transcendent and immanent, understanding and literature. There's more I, a new pilgrim finding his way in Bali, have yet to know.

The Son of Shiva and Parvati broke His ivory tusk to write the Mahabharata for Bhagavan Vyasa, the blind author of the sacred Hindu epic. It's another metaphor among many. Writing is creation and magic, the pen is like a wand or the immortal Breath, and in chanting the Word we give life to matter. In this land mantra is worship: the tongue is the extension of the heart, its bridge to the world of sound and speech. Imagine Vyasa dictating his epic to his amanuensis Ganesha and Ganesha writing the story in sacred Sanskrit script. We are confronted with metaphor upon metaphor. Ganesha is the guardian at the door, our beginning, the start of a journey, of life. Pray to Him before undertaking anything. The Balinese know this and that's why they are focused, not on the past or future but on the present, this very instant. They know that every breath, every step is a meditation. That is what they teach yoga students in the ashram and in ancient disciplines and religions: the present is the only thing we have, everything else is void of existence. In the rain, I say to myself, Yes, this is the key to happiness, detachment, sealing of the senses, the Self and Brahman. We can be aware even of the heart beating and its secret language if we train in mindfulness. The simple lesson of Ganesha is that wherever we are, every second, every minute, is a sacred moment where we begin again.

OM GAM GANAPATEI NAMAHA**

*Marina is a famous Russian psychic who has the power to see with her eyes closed or blindfolded. She has demonstrated this gift many times under laboratory condition. Her husband Nicolai taught me the method of developing the ability when we were in Bali.

** "Salutations to Thee, O Remover of Obstacles." Mantra of Ganesha.

37

Peppercorn Treatment in a Balinese Temple

I was in Bali for a week in February 2006, the guest of a prominent family who made wonderful silk scarves under the brand name Bin House. Obin, the proprietor, told me to see a healer up in an old Hindu temple. He had successfully treated a woman of breast cancer with herbs, she said. Obin said that the old priest had married a young woman, had several children, and was still active in the healing trade. The driver took me up north past the rice fields and rice terraces and volcanoes. Along the way, women in colorful Balinese dresses were going to temple with baskets of flowers balanced on their heads. Wedha, my Javanese guide, spoke to the guard at the gate, told me to pay a hundred thousand rupiahs, and we were directed to a spot in the temple courtyard. The money covered entrance, the lectures and a treatment of indeterminate nature and duration. Ganesha, the Elephant God, God of beginnings and literature, sat on an improvised altar, beside a bell and a dorje, while incense burned somewhere among the flowers and palm leaves. There were people ahead of us sitting in a semi-circle in front of the old man, foreigners from America and Germany, mostly young women wearing sarong. He smiled openly, his teeth and mouth red from a lifetime of chewing betel nut. He talked half in Indonesian, half in English, and whenever he paused somebody translated for him in English. A blonde woman stepped forward and lay down on a mat in the center of a brick platform. I could not hear what he was saying to her, it was just a murmur, he was gentle, stroking her shoulder and head as he talked or recited mantras. When it was my turn, he gave me a painful treatment using a wand in the shape of a snake, probing acupressure points I recognized from acupuncture school. Every single one hurt, especially along the Bladder line. What is the matter with me? I thought. He did not give a diagnosis of what was wrong. I stood up when he was done. When he noticed I was sniffing, he asked me if I wanted a treatment for my sinuses. Without thinking, I said yes. Well, he turned to his table — I did not see what he was doing — and when he came back, he asked me to close my eyes. He spit on my face. I heard laughter from the 10-odd western people who were there to study with him. He told me to keep my eyes closed for 10 minutes. Meanwhile, his saliva dribbled down my face. After a few minutes, I felt relieved and smelled the pepper-like scent of the herb. Was that Sichuan peppercorn, a warming herb in Chinese herbal pharmacopeia? I wiped the saliva off with a handkerchief. My sinuses were clear for several days. The wonders of traditional eastern folk medicine!

38

My Gecko

Wedged at the joint of the ceiling in a triangular corner,
my gecko does not have to turn to take a peek at me when
I sit on the chaise lounge just outside my bedroom. I am
writing about this lonely house at the edge of the rice fields
in Maya Ubud: how isolated it is, how vulnerable it looks
amid the bananas, durians, frangipani, coconuts. I see a white
butterfly fluttering along the trellis of flowers, a red dragonfly
flying from leaf to leaf in a secret benediction. A man scything
the tall grass is coughing. A piece of wildness at the end of a long
trail from the road, through a steel gate, a slow descent and a last
abrupt turn. At sundown the lamp, a beacon beside a spirit
house, glows in the gathering darkness. I want my gecko to start
its ritual of mantras, the sacred sounds of worship to the earth,
its tu-ko, tu-ko, tu-ko cries offer me the protection and blessing
of its trembling voice. Its invocation reaching farther than the trees
and the stars to the island of the gods and goddesses. I can hear
the roar of the tuktuks and the motorcycles, the song of a bird
and the echo of conversations across the stream. But I am alone here.
The jackfruit hanging 50 feet in the air at the end of a stem beckons.
Gecko of my childhood, my little Dragon, my green shaman, I heard
your chanting when I was half-awake in this big bed, your range
reaching me in my dreams, as I drifted into restful, hypnotic slumber
after a long flight from my home 4 hours away. You honor our planet,
you honor life, with your single notes. At night, at sunset, you never
fail to bow your head and for an Eternity shake my body with your
throaty syllables: I should join you in your daily regimen of reverence
to the sacred in the world. Mornings and evenings, I should bow
to the holy: The gifts of sun, moon, the greening leaves, the breeze
that touches me, the spirits I see wandering in the garden,

or moving through the glass of the bay windows that open into the porch, the blood that flows in my veins, a heart that pulses quietly through the channels of my mortal flesh. I should repeat the ancient mantras of my people:

Bari, bari, Apu.
Great Ancestor, give me protection.
Allow me and my loves to pass through
This narrow trail to our home
In the woods
Unharmed in life.
Bless me with my Gecko's sacred sound.
Om Shantih Shantih Shantih
Peace Peace Peace
Tu-Ko Tu-Ko Tu-ko

– Ubud, Bali, 2016

39

Bali Rain

Waiting an hour for the rain to fall:
it finally came in late afternoon.
Francesca was going through her yoga
asanas when I woke up in the living room.
Uma was in the bedroom
napping. The rest of the group
hadn't appeared for the seminar
on detachment, impermanence,
taboos, aggregates, memory
and the Self. We were stranded
by the rain.
In January the rain comes
every day to Bali.
These are hot days
but the rain comes
and falls for hours
at this time of the year
regardless. We are told the rain is a gift
from the gods of the sky
and the dry earth is thankful
for its blessing.
In the Philippines of my childhood, the rain
came in May, the month
of the flowers and the Flores
de Mayo festivals.
We children followed the local beauty queens
and their escorts, little
kids dressed up in white

as King Constantine, through
the streets of my hometown.
As a child of 6, I used to go out
and shower in the rain,
got my feet
wet and muddy as I ran
around the neighborhood
naked with my cousins.
Just now, at 73, with the rain
pouring heavy in the courtyard
of the temple at Jawaran Street,
this early afternoon,
I took off
my clothes, stepped into the open
patio in the yard, faced the wall
of black volcanic rocks in back,
and raised my head
and arms to the sky, water pouring
over me, washing
my crown, my eyes
and ears, my hands,
armpits,
thighs, feet,
my whole body,
as a single stick of incense
burned in the
darkness
of the altar
to Ganesha,
the god
of beginnings
and entrances.

Notes

"Fairy Child" — This is the posture I am holding on the front cover. I learned this old Shaolin/Buddhist Hung Kuen set, called "Fairy Child Praying to the Goddess of Mercy Guanyin," from two Chinese masters – Johnny Chiuten (Wong Fiak San) and Lao Kim (Goon Tiong) – in the Philippines in the 1960s when I was in my mid-20s. The origins of the form are obscure, but the choreography is clearly derived from a temple. Guanyin, the Bodhisattva of Compassion, evolved from Hindu tradition. As time passed, the original male figure was gradually transformed into a female figure in China, adopted by both Buddhist and Daoist devotees. The elaborate set shows a child at play, but the techniques combine deadly martial, aesthetic dance, and devotional gestures, employing more open yin hands than yang fists. It is indeed a rare form in the repertoire of martial arts. The word Fairy, or *Xian* in Chinese, refers to a person who lives in the mountain. There is no adequate translation in English, but contemporary usage renders the word *xian* as "immortal." This particular posture happens towards the end of the form. The Fairy Child, his back turned to the audience, is facing the statue of Guanyin. He does the "prayer or salutation" mudra 3 times. The posture is suggestive of the character for woman or nu and is often called "cross or scissor stance."

"Ling" — This is the calligraphy presented on page xv. *Ling* (second tone 靈) is a Chinese character that has been translated as "spirit." But something is lost in the translation because it means much more. Since it is composed of several radicals, it is difficult to translate with one word. There's a horizontal line that can mean one or perhaps heaven, another radical that shows a roof or a cloud and rain/yu, 3 mouths/kou below that, and at the bottom is a shaman/wu (2 figures for man or ren). Taken as a whole, and read from below, the character shows a shaman praying or doing a ritual to bring down the energy or Qi, or the blessing of Heaven. In Daoism, the 3 mouths or body openings stand for Fengfu (Warehouse of Wind), known also as Du Mai 16 (below the occiput); Bai Hui (Hundred Convergences or Meetings), known also as Du Mai 20 (at the top of the head); and Yintang (Esoteric Hall), located between the eyebrows. A Buddhist told me that the 3 mouths refer to the 3 Dantian or elixir fields. We can understand Ling as Heaven's response to the shamanic prayer.

"Bilocation" — The United States invaded the Philippines in 1898 on the pretext that it was saving the country from Spain and this was also part of the American Manifest Destiny. The colonization of the Philippines was alleged to have the intention of "Christianizing" and "civilizing" the Filipinos. During this racist war of conquest, many villages were burned, Filipinos were massacred and torture (like "water cure" and "rope cure") was rampant.

"Sulu" — Sulu is an island in southwest Philippines. In the 70s, during the reign of Ferdinand Marcos, Jolo, the capital, was bombed by the Philippine air force. The poem was written when the author saw a photograph of a child pushing a cart in the ruins of the city in 1974. It was part of a set of poems inspired by the piano composition, "Kinderszenen" (Scenes from Childhood), by Robert Schumann.

"Mattapoisett Neck Beach Spring Equinox Morning" — Spring Equinox is one of the most significant terrestrial events in Daoism. It is one of the Four Gates: it is believed that Heaven opens during the solstices and equinoxes and we can send our invocations to the Dao during those times. Spring is when the Dragons emerge from the waters of Winter, bringing thunder, rain and lightning. Spring is also the time for rebirth after the dead of Winter. It is when life emerges, ice melts and streams begin to flow, and nature is resurrected.

"Return" — There is a belief in Daoism that we return to our origins or source and that is the Dao. "Reversal is the way of the Dao," says verse 40 of the *Dao De Iing* (Book of Changes). In Daoism, the practitioner "reverses" many common practices, customs and traditions. In this process of inversion, there are practices that move the energy the "other way" — ascetism instead of indulgence, the sexual energy going up instead of down, breathing in the belly instead of in the chest, etc. *Ziran* means "natural," "effortless," or "spontaneous." It has also been translated as "suchness" or "things as they are." Along with *wu wei* or non-action, it is one of the main themes of the *Dao De Jing* and Daoism. This poem was written as part of the Poets Against the War protest, against the US invasion of Iraq and as a reaction to "Reinventing the World," a wonderful poem Mark Frutkin wrote at the time.

"The Old Calligrapher" — The victims of Hiroshima did not know what hit them. To describe the Bomb, the word "picadon" was coined. "Pica" means flash or flicker, and "don" means loud noise or explosion. Certain victims left shadows. Bodhidharma, the legendary first patriarch of Buddhism in China, also left his shadow on a rock close to the spot where he meditated for nine years. This rock is located near the Shaolin temple in Luoyang, Honan province. I first read this poem at the 40th anniversary commemoration sponsored by the Lehigh Valley Peace Council (LEPOCO) and the Interfaith Council at the Garden of Serenity in Bethlehem, Pennsylvania in 1985. The movie "Hiroshima, Mon Amour" by Alain Resnais and Margaret Duras, was the inspiration for it. I submitted the poem to the Lafayette Spring Poetry Festival in Easton, PA. June Jordan wrote to the author saying it is a "beautiful and gifted poem."

"Sword Dance in the Moonlight," "Return," "Cheng-Du Dawn" and "Meditation" — In Daoist practices, usually the focus is on the area behind the navel called *dan tian,* which literally means "elixir field." In this space qi/lifeforce is collected assuring the practitioner longevity and perhaps immortality. In Tai Ji Quan and the Sword Dance, the trajectory of the *qi* (lifeforce) is aligned with the Navel. The energies of yin (feminine) and yang (masculine) — Dragon and Phoenix are the usual representations — are mated in the process of meditation. The regimen is called *nei dan* or internal alchemy or the *Enlightenment of Kan and Li* (water and fire).

"Dragon," "Ascension," "North Star in Doi Saket," "At Marble Collegiate Church with Marla and Donald," "A Clearing in the Sky" — The concept of ascension is pervasive in the East. It is believed that the body is composed of the *jing* (essence), *qi* (lifeforce) and *shen* (spirit), the traditional *san bao* (three treasures) or *san cai* (elemental trinity). The world is not just composed of matter. Nature itself possesses this character. Hence, there is often the phenomenon of ascension: humans, animals and objects transforming into energy or spirit. Sometimes the qi (energy) is drawn into or projected from the navel, which is called the *Shen Que* or "Gate of the Spirit." The dragon and crane are the mythical animals that symbolize Ascension in Daoist cosmology.

"A Clearing in the Sky" — The wedding of Al and Laura 25 years ago was featured in Martha Stewart's wedding magazine edition under the title, "A Clearing in the Woods." Al and Laura have two children – Isabel, 22, and Ava, 18. They live in Frenchtown, New Jersey.

"Island Shaman" — Here the amulet, or *anting-anting*, is a "double crucifix." There is a crucified Christ on each side of the cross. It is worn by healers, martial artists and *arnisadores* (practitioners of stick-fighting) in the country. It is believed to protect against evil attacks from the front and back.

"Dream on Wat Phra That Doi Suthep" — Wat Phrathat Doi Suthep is a Buddhist temple on top of a mountain in Chiang-mai, Thailand.

"Dream on Huashan" — Huashan (Flower Mountain) is a Daoist sacred mountain in China.

"Thinking of Li Bai" — This alludes to the farewell poem of the Tang Dynasty poet laureate, "Dreaming of Wandering through Tien-Mu Mountain." Along with **"Sword Dance in the Moonlight,"** this work mentions Li Bai's habit of dropping his poems like peach blossoms on a stream.

"Company" — Lapu-Lapu was the chieftain of the island of Mactan in Central Philippines. He is considered the first Filipino to resist foreign invasion.

"Longhushan Idyll" — According to Zhang Sanfeng, the founder of Tai Ji Quan, there are five practices of self-cultivation: 1. Doing sword dance in the moonlight because it would enliven the spirit; 2. Practicing Tai Ji Quan at night to improve vital essence; 3. Climbing a mountain to cultivate qi; 4. Reading the scriptures on stormy nights to illuminate the mind; and 5. Meditating at midnight to enlighten one's nature. See *Tai Ji Quan Treatise: Attributed to the Song Dynasty Daoist priest Zhang Sanfeng* by Stuart Alve Olson (Valley Spirit Arts).

"Chichen Itza Mexico" — There is a sacred pond or cenote in the complex. In ancient times devotees offered precious objects and humans, dropping them in the water. At the equinoxes (equal day and night) the god Kukulkan/Quetzalcoatl in the form of a snake was supposed to descend the pyramid. I made pilgrimages to Chichen Itza in the 1980s.

"Meditation" — This poem is based on the Daoist meditation Xiao Zhou Tian or Small Heavenly Circle (also popularly called Microcosmic Orbit).

"Meditating on Ganesha" — My earliest encounter with Hindu culture was in February 2006 when I traveled to Bali for the first time. Since then I have been to Bali 5 times. It was in 2012, however, that I began my serious study of Hinduism. I sat in on the private lessons taught by a 93-year old Hindu priest in Bali during the initiation of David Verdesi. I began reading the literature — *Bhagavad Gita, Upanishads*, the *Yoga Sutras* of Patanjali — and collecting artifacts. This piece describes my first encounter with Lord Ganesha. I started to listen to mantras and lectures from ashrams on the internet. There is so much more to learn.

Acknowledgments

These poems appeared in the following journals and anthologies:

"Tai Ji Quan": an earlier version of this poem was first published in the anthology "Pinoy Poetics" (Meritage Press). I wrote the poem in response to the poem "Alignment" by Luis Cabalquinto.

"Sword Dance in the Moonlight": APAJ Journal (Asian American Writers Workshop).

"Dragon (Winter 1995)": "Flippin' – Filipinos on America" (Asian American Writers Workshop:1996)). This was the first anthology to publish my poetry.

"Company," "A Clearing in the Sky," and "At Marble Collegiate Church with Marla and Donald" in Nyuroasian Anthology (Asian American Writers Workshop).

"At the Nursing Home with Dad" in Father Poems (Anvil Publication).

"Treating Father with Acupuncture" and "Watching the Incense Burn: Instructions for a Devotional" in Marsh Hawk Review.

"At West Lake – After Bai Ju-Yi," "Cheng-Du Dawn" and "Renga," were first published in Our Own Voice, an internet literary magazine.

"Renga" was written sometime at the millennium. Nadine Sarreal was writing from Singapore and I was writing from Lake Harmony in Pennsylvania. Nadine is the author of an acclaimed book of short stories. She lives in Manila now.

Some of these poems were originally published in the chapbook "Du Fu's Cottage and Other Poems" (1995) and in my website.

My heartfelt gratitude first of all to my family, especially Lolit, Albert and Norman, and Laura for always being there for me; Lou and April Fernandez for their first class hospitality; Malula Longo and Janet Lehman and Cathy Sanders and Melina Salerno, friends in Boston who always have a place for me in their home and life; Len Roberts, my poetry mentor and friend, for his invaluable guidance; June Jordan for her kind critique of "The Old Calligrapher"; Manny Maramara for his computer expertise and support; to my masters Lao Kim and Johnny Chiuten in Shaolin Hong Kuen, Chan Bun Te, Gin Soon Chu and Vincent F. Chu in Classical Yang Family Tai Ji Quan, and Mantak Chia and Jeffrey Yuen in Daoism, Ou Wen Wei in Pangu Mystical Qigong; Mark Wiley for his friendship and work; David Verdesi, my cicerone through many journeys in unknown lands and lineages; my brothers Roland, Danilo and Florante Navarro, cousin Letty Espinelli and generous colleagues and friends Ed Maranan, Temy Rivera, Dr. Jopet Laraya, Vic Ramos, Karen Borla, Mike Arsenault, Lee Holden, Amirah Snaith and Josue "Sonny" Villa and the kababayan who have enriched my life in many ways ; Guru and Suh Bose and Bill and Diane Craft for going out of their way to keep me company and lending me a listening ear whenever I needed it; and my patient student Annie Sollestre and INAM PHILIPPINES for organizing my work over the years in my country of birth. Special thanks to Filipino poets Eileen Tabios, Eric Gamalinda, Luis Francia, Nick Carbo, Bino Realuyo, Alfred Yuson, Jimmy Abad and Luisa Carino Igloria. I should also thank the many extraordinary healers I have met – among them, Chaiyuth Priyasith in Thailand, John Chang in Java, Jiang Feng and Xong Kuan in Huangshan and Guiling Tinga in Bantayan Island who have all passed away. Last but not least, thanks to my granddaughters Isabel and Ava who have always inspired me in my work and have strengthened my hope for the future.

About the Author

Rene J. Navarro is a licensed acupuncturist, herbalist, martial artist, Daoist teacher, healer, essayist, poet and alchemist. His poetry and essays have been published in the US, Europe and Asia. He has taught in four continents. He was a disciple of Grandmasters Lao Kim and Johnny Chiuten in Shaolin/Buddhist Hung Kuen studying fist and weapons forms including Tiger-Dragon Fist, Plum Blossom/Flower Fist, Fairy Child Praying to the Goddess of Mercy Guanyin, Flower Staff, Broadsword, Straight Sword, 5 Sectional Steel Whip, Hoe, and Guandao. He is a senior student of Grandmaster Gin Soon Chu and 6th generation practitioner of Classical Yang Family Tai Ji Quan with intensive training in the 108 movement solo fist form, Dao/Broadsword (2 sets), Jian/Straight sword (2 sets), Staff-Spear, Sansou (2-person sparring set), Push Hands and the Tai Ji Quan Chang Quan (the old form of Tai Ji Quan). He is a senior instructor of the Universal Healing Tao under Grandmaster Mantak Chia certified to teach Microcosmic Orbit, Tai chi chi kung, Healing Love (Daoist sexology), Chi Nei Tsang internal organs massage, Fusion of the 5 Elements and Kan and Li (neidan/internal alchemy). His teachers include Jeffrey Yuen (Chinese medicine and classics), David Verdesi (Thunder Path), Kiiko Matsumoto (Japanese acupuncture), Yao Zhang (Chinese herbs), Ou Wen Wei (Pangu Mystical Qigong), Johnny F. Chiuten, Guiling Tinga and Amante "Mat" Marinas (arnis de mano) and Vincent F. Chu and Chan Bun Te (Yang Family Tai Ji Quan). He holds a Bachelor of Arts (MLQ University), a Law degree (University of the Philippines), a diploma in acupuncture and a certificate in

Chinese herbalism (New England School of Acupuncture). In an earlier incarnation, he worked as a lawyer representing indigent clients in NY. He lives in the foothills of the Appalachian mountains, Pennsylvania, USA.

"Rene is an amazingly powerful, gentle and magical being."
– Comment from a student.

For more information, please go to his website:
www.renenavarro.org

www.ingramcontent.com/pod-product-compliance
Lightning Source LLC
Chambersburg PA
CBHW031143090426
42738CB00008B/1201

* 9 7 8 1 9 4 3 1 5 5 3 4 7 *